Hurricanes!

by Lorraine Jean Hopping
Illustrated by Jody Wheeler

Hello Reader!

SCHOLASTIC INC. Cartwheel B·O·O·K·S ®
New York   Toronto   London   Auckland   Sydney

Chapter 1

Through the Wall

Pretend you are a pilot.
You are flying
as high as the clouds.
All you see is
a wall of darkness.
It is nighttime.
Thunder booms.
Lightning flashes.
Your plane jumps up and
down, and side to side.
You feel like popcorn
in the making.

You have orders
to follow.
You must fly
into the center
of a hurricane.
Then you must
fly out again.
Seven times!

Wes Bennett got those orders
on September 17, 1989.
On that day, a hurricane
named Hugo was heading
toward the east coast
of the United States.
But Wes was not scared.
Flying through hurricanes
is his job.
Wes is a Storm Tracker.

Storm Trackers measure
the size, temperature,
and location of a hurricane.
They take these readings
from *inside* the storm.

Their job is not
an easy one.
Hurricanes are huge masses
of spinning winds
that start out over the sea.

They are packed
with lightning, rain,
and power.
Every minute, a hurricane
releases as much power
as a hydrogen bomb!

eye

As soon as they got their orders,
Wes Bennett and his crew
flew off to meet Hugo.
They headed for Hugo's
eye, its center.
But first they had to get
through the storm's
feeder bands.
These are the outer arms
of the hurricane.
They make the storm look
like a giant pinwheel.

Each arm is a long line
of storm clouds.
Sheets of rain pour down
from these clouds.
They flash with lightning
and boom with thunder.
The winds are fast and strong.
There is no way for Storm Trackers
to avoid these feeder bands.

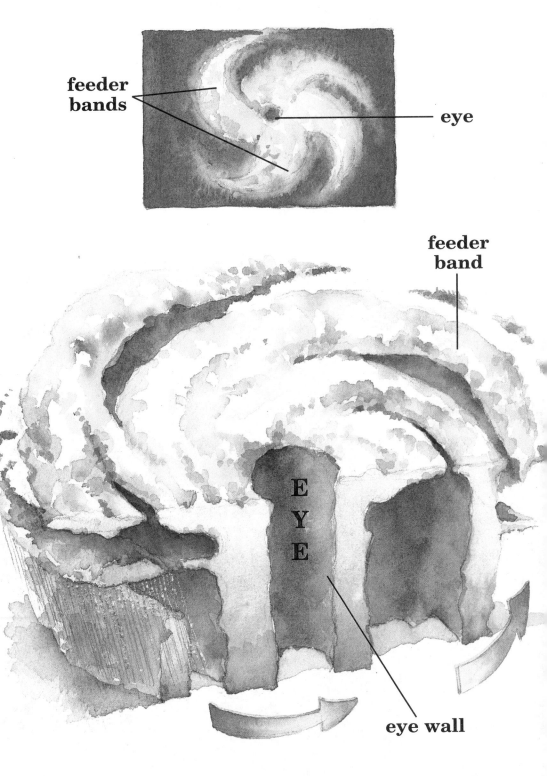

feeder
bands

eye

feeder
band

E
Y
E

eye wall

When the Storm Trackers
entered a feeder band,
it was pitch dark.
Then lightning lit the sky
near the plane.
The flash of light
revealed a wall
of black clouds.

Wes couldn't see where
he was flying.

He had to fly by reading
the instruments.
The instruments told him
the plane was 10,000 feet high.
The left wing was pointing
into the hurricane's wind.
And the nose was pointing
at Hugo's eye.
So far, so good!

But then, the plane
hit the eye wall,
a tall wall of clouds
around the eye.
It is where the
hurricane winds spin
the fastest.
They can reach 180 miles
per hour!

Sometimes, these winds
toss a plane right out
of the hurricane.

"Planes can turn
only so fast,"
Wes explained.
"The high winds change
direction suddenly and
throw you out."

When that happens,
the plane has to circle
around and try again.

Luckily, Wes and
his crew were able to slip
inside Hurricane Hugo.
But not without a scare.

The plane bounced
so hard that
the seat belts hurt.
The instruments went
out of whack
for a few seconds.
Wes fought to keep
his hands and feet
on the controls.

Then the jolting stopped.
In an instant,
the Storm Trackers broke
through the tall wall
of clouds.
They were inside Hugo's
calm, clear eye.

Chapter 2

Inside the Eye

From inside the eye,
Hugo looked like
a football stadium
made of beautiful,
silver storm clouds.

Like bleacher seats, the clouds
rose from the ocean in layers.
They were more than
four miles high.
The ocean formed the flat
"football field."
The waves were small
and calm.

17

Some hurricane "stadiums"
have a dome of clouds
above the eye.
Hugo did not.
The Storm Trackers could see
clear to the stars.
A full moon lit the eye
of Hurricane Hugo.

But not all was calm and clear
in Hugo's eye.
Wes Bennett felt dizzy.
He couldn't tell which
way was up.

More important, he wasn't
sure which way was down.
The instruments showed
one thing.
Wes's body told him the opposite.

"My co-pilot was watching me
to make sure I didn't listen
to my body," Wes said. "I
followed the instruments,
even though they didn't seem
right."

But the instruments *were*
right.
Wes kept the plane
inside the eye
for several uneasy minutes.
That was long enough
for the weather experts
to drop a box
out of the plane.

This box held weather
instruments.
It floated by parachute
down to the sea.
As it dropped,
the instruments measured
the temperature and
other conditions
in the heart
of the storm.

Still dizzy, Wes now had
to fly out of the hurricane.
There was only one way out.
He had to go back
through the windy eye wall.
Then he had to cross
the stormy feeder bands again.

Did Wes head home?
Not a chance!
He and the crew flew
through Hurricane Hugo
seven times, as ordered.
Their data went to the
National Hurricane Center
in Florida.
The data helped scientists
predict Hugo's deadly path.

The day of the flight,
Hugo swept across the island
of St. Croix in the Caribbean Sea.
Dozens of islanders lost
their lives.
Thousands lost their homes.
Four days later,
on September 21, 1989,
Hugo slammed into South Carolina.

All hurricanes create
storm surges.
A storm surge is
a sudden rise
in the water level
of the ocean.

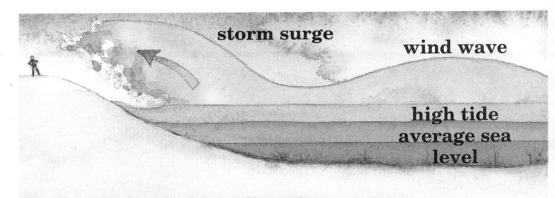

storm surge

wind wave

high tide

average sea
level

Hugo's storm surge was
20 feet high.
It washed away houses and
bridges.
Winds gusted to 150 miles
per hour.
Cars flipped over.
Boats crashed ashore.
Trees were flattened
into giant toothpicks.

In all, Hugo killed 504 people.
But millions survived.
Some people took shelter
in schools and other buildings.
Others had evacuated, or
cleared out of town, hours
before the storm.
Reports on the radio
had warned them.
The Storm Trackers helped make
these reports possible.

Chapter 3

A Hurricane Is Born

In the Atlantic Ocean,
hurricane season is
from June to November.
Storm tracking begins
even before a hurricane
is a hurricane.
The giant storms
start out at sea
as weaker areas
of circling winds.
These winds are called
tropical depressions.

The winds spin slowly
and are spread out over
a wide area.
Storm Trackers meet
these first spinning winds
head-on.

They measure the temperature
of these winds —
both inside and out.
The warmer the center
of the storm,
the stronger it is.

Storm Trackers take
other readings as well.
They look closely
at the eye.
It may be tiny, tight,
and as round as
a doughnut hole.
If so, watch out!
This means the winds
may spin into a
tropical storm.
This happens one out
of ten times.
The other nine times,
the spinning winds die out.

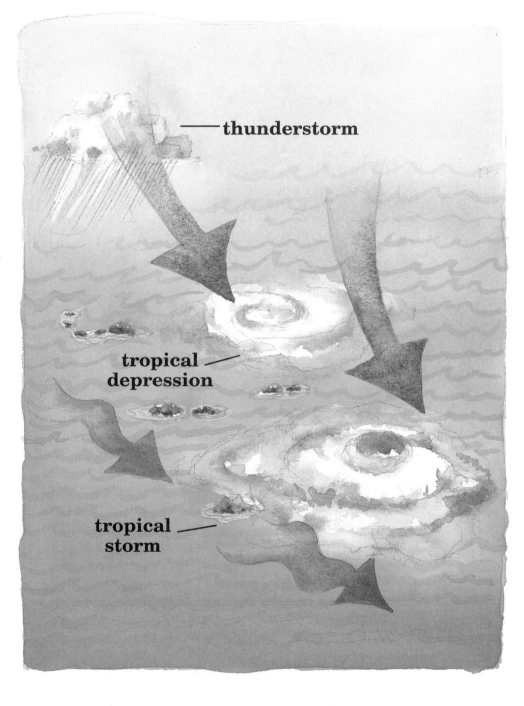

thunderstorm

tropical
depression

tropical
storm

 trade winds

 low pressure
wave

A tropical storm is
like a hurricane,
only weaker.
The winds blow up
to 73 miles per hour.
In the Atlantic Ocean,
a tropical storm usually heads
from east to west,
toward the United States.
Storm Trackers watch
this kind of storm
carefully.

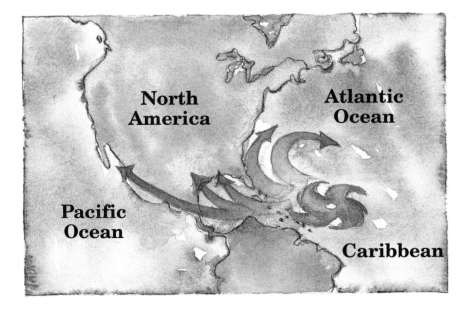

Just as a car needs
fuel to keep running,
so does a tropical storm.
Its fuel isn't gas,
though.
It is the warm,
wet air that rises
from the sea.
The water temperature
must be above 81 degrees
Fahrenheit.
If the water temperature
is below 81 degrees
Fahrenheit, the storm
runs out of energy
and dies.

If it is above 81 degrees
Fahrenheit, the winds
spin faster.

They form a tighter and
tighter circle.
The storm grows
stronger.
If the winds reach
74 miles per hour,
a hurricane is born.
The weather service
gives it
a hurricane name,
such as Alison or Barry.
A name that starts
with *A* means
it is the first hurricane
of the season.
A *B* name is for
the second hurricane,
and so on.

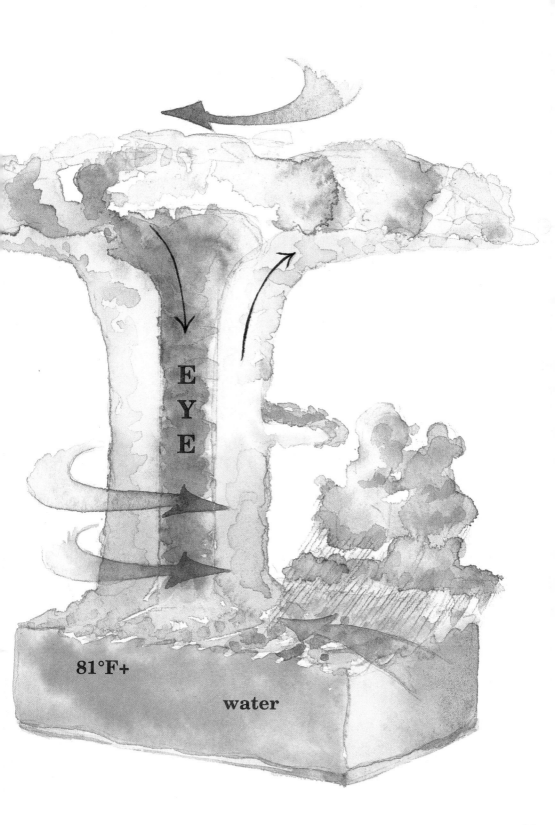

EYE

81°F+

water

Chapter 4

Zigzag Storms

Hurricanes do not all follow
the same route.
There is no "hurricane
highway" in the sky.
These storms zig, zag, and
even turn around and
go the other way!

"The biggest faker
I can remember
was Hurricane Elena
in 1985," Wes Bennett said.

"It was supposed
to hit my area,
Biloxi, Mississippi.
But then it hung a right
and moved toward Florida.
People in Biloxi thought
they were off the hook.
Then Elena turned back
to the west.
It hit Biloxi!"

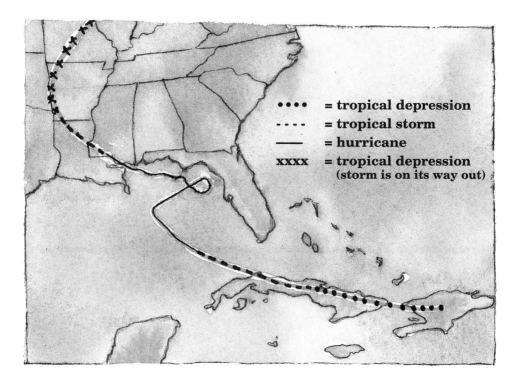

•••• = tropical depression
- - - - = tropical storm
—— = hurricane
xxxx = tropical depression
(storm is on its way out)

These zigs and zags
make a hurricane's path
hard to predict.
But experts do have
a few guidelines to follow:

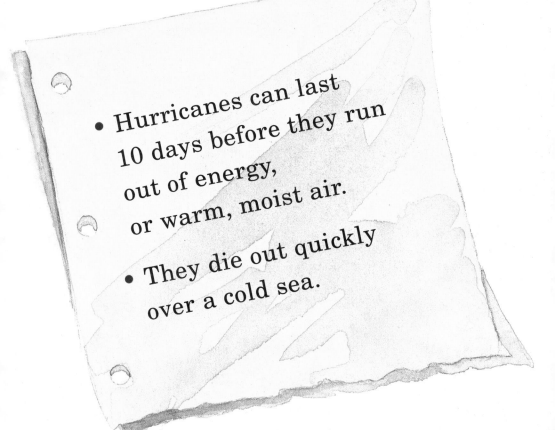

- Hurricanes can last
10 days before they run
out of energy,
or warm, moist air.

- They die out quickly
over a cold sea.

- Hurricanes never form on the equator, and they never cross it.

- Hurricanes are slow. They travel about 15 miles per hour over water. Bicycles can go faster than that.

- Hurricanes usually slow down when they hit land, especially mountains.

Hurricanes may be slow,
but their winds spin
very, very fast.
Imagine a street-cleaning
machine.
The brushes scrub
in fast circles,
like the hurricane winds.
But the machine itself,
like the storm, moves slowly
down the street.

Every 12 to 24 hours,
Storm Trackers fly
through those winds
to collect data.
Their data ends up
in computers at the
National Hurricane Center
in Florida.

The scientists
at the center
use their computers
to carefully watch
the progress of the storm.

The scientists also
collect data
from other sources.
One source is weather
satellites.

Chapter 5

Sky-high Views

Since the 1960s,
satellites have watched
hurricanes from space.
But satellites can't
give us all of the data
we need.
For example, in 1969, a satellite
spotted Hurricane Camille
in the Gulf of Mexico.
The storm looked small
from space.
People didn't think
much of it.

Storm Trackers found out
otherwise.
Unlike satellites, their view
wasn't sky high.
They saw Hurricane Camille
from the inside.

Yes, Camille was small.
But the eye was tiny
and round.
It had no holes or gaps
in the sides.
That meant Camille had
a lot of power.
Its winds hit 180 miles
per hour — the fastest
possible speed
for a hurricane!

People were warned.
They left their homes.
Whole towns were cleared out.
Camille ruined 75,000 homes.
More than 250 people died
in the storm.
Many more people would have died
if they had not fled.
The lesson was that
satellites alone cannot
track hurricanes.

They can't see how fast
the winds spin or exactly
where the eye is.
Only Storm Trackers
can do that.
Better tracking has
reduced the hurricane
death toll in the
Western Hemisphere.
Countries with poor
warning systems are not
so lucky.

Bangladesh is next to
the Indian Ocean in Asia.
About 300,000 people died there
in a cyclone in 1970.
Hurricanes are called
cyclones in the Indian Ocean.
It was the deadliest storm
on record.
In 1991, another storm
killed about 100,000 people
in Bangladesh.

One year later, in 1992,
Hurricane Andrew struck
the United States.
This powerful storm hit
Florida and Louisiana.
It was the most expensive
storm on record.

Andrew destroyed $10 billion
worth of property.
Yet only 52 people died.
Andrew proved that tracking
storms can't save property.
But it can save lives.
And that's why Storm Trackers
stay on the job.

"After a twelve-hour flight,
I'm dog-tired," Wes Bennett
said. "I go home and turn
on the TV.
"The weather report says,
'Aircraft have pinpointed
the location of the storm.'
It tells people to clear out.
I think, 'That's me.
I did that. I save lives!' "

Hurricane Safety Tips

- Check that flashlights and radios are always in good working condition.

- Always have a stock of fresh drinking water, canned food, and warm blankets on hand.

- If a hurricane is approaching, keep calm and stay with your family.

- Listen to the radio or watch the TV for storm conditions and evacuation information.

- When officials tell your family to clear out, do it.